PRESIDENT

By Jacqueline Laks Gorman
Reading consultant: Susan Nations, M.Ed.,
author/literacy coach/consultant in literacy development

Gareth Stevens
PUBLISHING

Please visit our web site at www.garethstevens.com
For a free color catalog describing our list of high-quality books,
call 1-800-542-2595 (USA) or 1-800-387-3178 (Canada). Our fax: 1-877-542-2596

Library of Congress Cataloging-in-Publication Data
    Gorman, Jacqueline Laks, 1955–
       President / by Jacqueline Laks Gorman ; reading consultant, Susan Nations.
         p. cm. — (Know your government)
       Includes bibliographical references and index.
       ISBN-10: 1-4339-0095-5 ISBN-13: 978-1-4339-0095-2 (lib. bdg.)
       ISBN-10: 1-4339-0123-4 ISBN-13: 978-1-4339-0123-2 (softcover)
       1. Presidents—United States—Juvenile literature. I. Title.
    JK517.G68   2008
    352.230973—dc22   2008033378

Executive Managing Editor: Lisa M. Herrington
Editors: Brian Fitzgerald and Barbara Kiely Miller
Creative Director: Lisa Donovan
Senior Designer: Keith Plechaty
Photo Researchers: Charlene Pinckney and Diane Laska-Swanke
Publisher: Keith Garton

Photo credits: cover & title page Emmanuel Dunand/AFP/Getty Images; p. 5 © John Zich/zrImages/Corbis;
p. 6 © EyeWire; p. 7 White House photo by Joyce Boghosian; p. 9 Ron Sachs-Pool/Getty Images; p. 10 George
Bush Presidential Library; p. 11 White House photo by Paul Morse; p. 12 White House photo by Tina Hager;
p. 13 © Tel Or Beni/GPO/Getty Images; p. 15 Jeff Chiu/AP; p. 16 Jim Bourg, Pool/AP; p. 17 Doug Mills/AP;
p. 19 © Stock Montage, Inc.; p. 20 © North Wind Picture Archives; p. 21 © Marie Hansen/Time & Life Pictures/
Getty Images.

Printed in the United States of America

1 2 3 4 5 6 7 8 9 10 09 08

Cover Photo: Barack Obama was elected the 44th president of the United States in 2008.

TABLE OF CONTENTS

Words that appear in the glossary are printed in **boldface** type the first time they appear in the text.

CHAPTER 1

Who Is the President?

The president is the leader of the United States. He is a leader in the world, too. The president is very powerful. Today, people still talk about what presidents did many years ago.

Voters **elect**, or choose, the president every four years. More than 300 million people live in the United States. The president works for all of them! He decides what is best for the country.

In 2008, Barack Obama became the first African American to be elected president. His family joined him for his victory speech.

The president lives in the White House. The White House is at 1600 Pennsylvania Avenue in Washington, D.C.

The president lives and works at the White House. He works in the Oval Office. The White House is in Washington, D.C., the capital of the United States. The capital is the center of government.

The president travels on a special plane called *Air Force One*. He also has a helicopter called *Marine One*.

Trained people protect the president and his family. These guards are called the Secret Service.

Marine One often lands on the lawn at the White House.

CHAPTER 2

What Does the President Do?

The president has one of the hardest jobs in the world. He has to lead the country during good times and bad. The president picks many men and women to help him do his job.

The president's top helpers are called his **Cabinet**. People in the Cabinet run 15 government departments. They work in education, health, and other important areas. The president meets with his Cabinet often. They talk about ways to fix problems in the country.

President George W. Bush (center) often met with his Cabinet to talk about the country's problems.

President George H. W. Bush signed a bill into law in July 1990. The new law helped people with disabilities.

The president also works with Congress. Congress is the part of government that makes laws. Members of Congress write **bills**, or ideas for new laws. The president must sign a bill before it becomes a law. The president makes sure that laws are carried out.

Every year, the president makes an important speech, or address, to Congress and the rest of the country. He tells everyone how the country is doing. He also talks about his plans for solving the country's problems.

President George W. Bush gave his yearly address to Congress in January 2006.

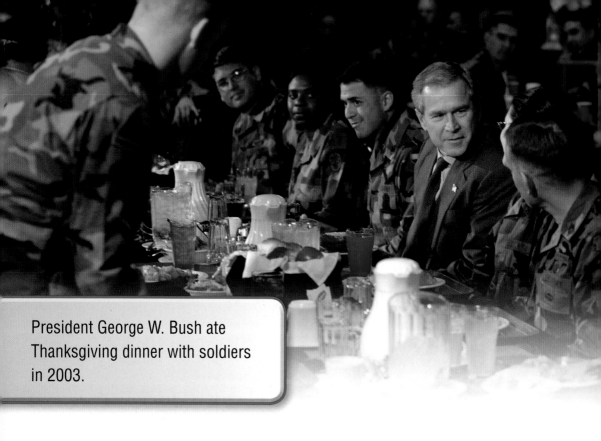

President George W. Bush ate Thanksgiving dinner with soldiers in 2003.

The president is the commander in chief of the **military**. The military protects the country. The Army, Navy, Air Force, Marines, and Coast Guard are all parts of the military. Congress must vote before the president sends the military into battle.

The president decides how the United States works with other countries. He often meets with other world leaders. He can make **treaties**, or agreements, with them. The president may also decide to give aid to countries in need.

President Jimmy Carter (center) met with the leaders of Egypt and Israel in 1978. He helped them make a peace treaty between their countries.

CHAPTER 3

How Does a Person Become President?

To become president, a person must be at least 35 years old. He or she must be a **citizen** born in the United States. He or she must have lived in the United States for at least 14 years. Voters elect the president every four years. A president can serve only two **terms**, or periods in office.

People who run for office are called **candidates**. Most candidates are from one of two main **political parties**: the Democratic Party and the Republican Party. The two main parties hold big meetings called **conventions** to pick their candidates for president.

At the 2008 Democratic convention, people cheered for their candidate, Barack Obama.

Each candidate has a **running mate**. That person will become vice president if the candidate wins. The candidates travel across the country. They give speeches and talk to voters. They have **debates** about important issues.

Millions of people watched a debate between John McCain (left) and Barack Obama (right) in September 2008.

Finally, Election Day arrives in November. People all over the country vote. In January, the new president takes over. He makes a special promise called the **Oath of Office**. The new president moves into the White House with his or her family.

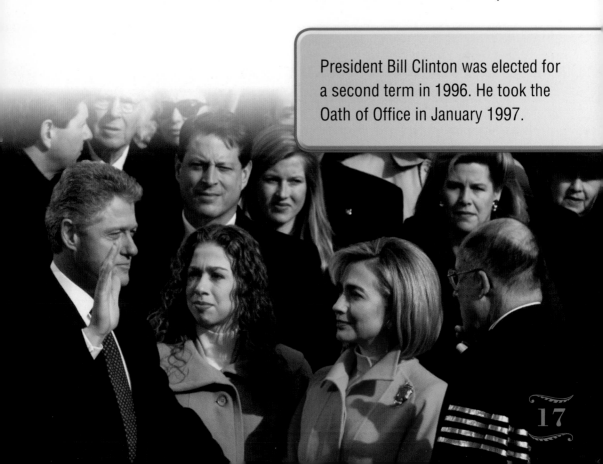

President Bill Clinton was elected for a second term in 1996. He took the Oath of Office in January 1997.

CHAPTER 4

Famous Presidents

Many presidents have done great things. They became part of history. George Washington was a war hero. He helped Americans win their freedom from Great Britain. In 1789, he became the first president of the United States.

Thomas Jefferson wrote the Declaration of Independence in 1776. It declared the country's freedom from Great Britain. In 1801, Jefferson became the third president. As president, he helped the United States double in size.

George Washington was elected president on January 7, 1789. He took the Oath of Office on April 30.

President Abraham Lincoln made speeches that helped people stay strong during the Civil War.

Abraham Lincoln was the 16th president. He led the nation during the Civil War (1861–1865). He ended slavery. He was a brave leader when the nation needed him. Lincoln was shot and killed in 1865.

Franklin Roosevelt served longer than any other president. He became president in 1933. At the time, many people were poor and had no jobs.

Roosevelt helped people find jobs. He also gave the country hope. That is a sign of all great presidents.

Franklin Roosevelt was president from 1933 to 1945. He often talked to the people on the radio.

Glossary

bills: written plans for new laws

Cabinet: a group of people who lead government departments. Cabinet members work for the president.

candidates: people who are running for office

citizen: an official member of a country who has certain rights, such as voting

conventions: big meetings at which political parties choose their candidate for president

debates: formal arguments between candidates about important issues

elect: to choose a leader by voting

military: a country's armed forces

Oath of Office: the promise the president makes to uphold the nation's laws and lead the country

political parties: groups of people who have similar beliefs and ideas

running mate: a person running for vice president

terms: set periods of time that a person serves in office

treaties: agreements made between countries

To Find Out More

Books

Don't Know Much About the Presidents. Kenneth C. Davis
(HarperCollins, 2003)

So You Want to Be President? Judith St. George (Philomel, 2008)

The White House. Places in American History (series). Susan Ashley
(Weekly Reader Books, 2004)

Web Sites

President for a Day
pbskids.org/democracy/presforaday
This site lets you become the president and plan your busy schedule.

White House Kids
www.whitehouse.gov/kids
This site has biographies of the president and the first lady, a tour of
the White House, and more.

Index

About the Author

Jacqueline Laks Gorman is a writer and an editor. She grew up in New York City. She has worked on many kinds of books and has written several children's series. She lives with her husband, David, and children, Colin and Caitlin, in DeKalb, Illinois. She registered to vote when she turned 18 and votes in every election.